CW01192447

Belfast's Lost Tramways

by
Mike Maybin

The horse trams were converted to electric traction in two stages. The southern routes, including Lisburn Road, were opened on 29 November 1905, with the remainder of the services beginning on 5 December. This photograph was taken on the Lisburn Road to celebrate the last of the old horse cars. By this stage the entire fleet had been upgraded to three-windowed lower saloons, with improved interior 'Lincrusta' roof panels, and had their destination boxes adorned with the words of the 'The Lifeboat Rule is [destination] "Women and Children First"'. The terrace of houses to the right remains largely intact, although all have ground floor shop fronts. The houses nearest the camera on the right have been sympathetically remodelled into the Chelsea Wine Bar. The traction poles for the overhead power wires are in place. The entire conversion, including the construction of several major extensions, was carried out in the record time of just over eleven months. The Corporation had every right to a little quiet satisfaction in this achievement, given that most of the track had to be relaid, 170 new cars bought and stabled, Sandy Row, Falls Park, Antrim Road, Knock and Mountpottinger Depots had to be converted from horse to electric traction, Shore Road Depot and a new generating station needed to be constructed, and the existing service had to continue to run as normal!

Text © Mike Maybin, 2003.
First published in the United Kingdom, 2003,
by Stenlake Publishing
Telephone / Fax: 01290 551122
Printed by Cordfall Ltd, Glasgow, G21 2QA

ISBN 1 84033 277 8

The publishers regret that they cannot supply copies of any pictures featured in this book.

All photographs in this book are from the Des Quail collection.

The photographs by W.A. Camwell, on pages 31, 34, 36, 38, 41 (lower), 44 and the back cover, appear by permission of the National Tramway Museum.

FURTHER READING

The books listed below were used by the author during his research. None of them are available from Stenlake Publishing Ltd. Those interested in finding out more are advised to contact their local bookshop or reference library.

Belfast Corporation Transport Fleet List, P.S.V. Circle, 1968.
Bombs on Belfast, Belfast Telegraph, 1941.
Brett, C. E. B., *Buildings of Belfast 1700–1914*, Friars Bush Press, 1985 .
Hunter and Ludgate, *Gone but not Forgotten*, RPSI and ITT, 1979.
Larmour, P., *Belfast – An Illustrated Architectural Guide*, Friars Bush Press, 1987 .
Maybin, J. M., *Belfast Corporation Tramways 1905–54*, Light Railway Transport League, 1980.
Maybin, J. M., *A Nostalgic Look at Belfast Trams*, Silverlink Publishing, 1994.
Newham, A., *Cavehill & Whitewell Tramway*, Tramway Review Nos. 61–63, Light Railway Transport League.
Patton, M., *Central Belfast – A Historical Gazetteer*, Ulster Architectural Heritage Society, 1993.
Walker and Dixon, *No Mean City*, Friars Bush Press, 1983.

The official Belfast Corporation Archives held in the Public Record Office, local newspapers – the *Belfast Telegraph* and the *Belfast Newsletter* – and the excellent collection of Belfast Street Directories held in the Belfast and Linenhall Libraries were also consulted.

To operate the new electric service, Belfast City Tramways ordered 170 cars from J.G. White and Co. of London, who sub-let the contract for new cars to the Brush Electrical Engineering Co. of Loughborough at a cost of £586 per car. They were shipped to Belfast in the autumn of 1905 and this picture shows the lower deck of one of the new trams. They were 28 feet (approximately 8.6 metres) long and seated fifty-four passengers, of which twenty-two were accommodated downstairs and thirty-two on the top deck. The vehicles were delivered with ornate metal work corner pieces and a monogram of the BCT initials on either side of the of city crest. The city motto – *Pro Tanto Quid Retribuamus* – can be loosely translated as 'What return shall we make for so much'. Long-suffering ratepayers have been known to take a different view!

INTRODUCTION

In the latter half of the nineteenth century Belfast was the fastest growing town in the United Kingdom. Its main industries were shipbuilding, machine manufacturing and linen production. To service these expanding factories and warehouses, thousands of workers' houses were built along the arteries of the Shankill, Crumlin, Falls and Newtownards roads and it soon became necessary to build horse tramways to link the workers with their employment.

On 28 August 1872 the Belfast Street Tramways Company (BST) opened their first line from Castle Place to Botanic Gardens. It was immediately successful and was followed by extensions to other areas of the 'City' (as Belfast was proclaimed in 1888).

However, by 1881 poor management had produced major problems and a new manager, Andrew Nance, replaced the hapless Mr Totten. Nance was young, energetic and enthusiastic, and, to use a current business phrase, he 'turned the company round'. The system continued to expand and by the 1890s had reached most of the then built-up areas.

In 1881 a separate company built and operated a line between the village of Glengormley and the BST terminus at Chichester Park on the Antrim Road. The Cavehill & Whitewell Tramway (C&W), as it was known, enjoyed a separate existence until acquired by Belfast City Tramways in 1911.

Residents in the Ligoniel and Belmont districts were keen to have tramways in their areas, but the BST, always financially cautious, agreed only on condition that separate companies be established to build these lines, for which the BST paid a rental fee. The BST supplied the staff, cars and horses, retained the fares, and operated the lines integrally with their own.

In 1905 the entire system, with the exception of the C&W, was taken over by the Belfast Corporation and electrified. At the same time a number of extensions were built. In 1913, and again in the early 1920s, further extensions were undertaken and the basic route pattern, which forms the core of Citybus operations today, was established.

In 1926 the legislation changed and private motorbus operators switched from mainly country operations to compete with the Corporation trams. For almost six months, between June and December of 1928, the competition was fierce and the trams lost a lot of money and customers to the new, fast and convenient buses. Samuel Carlisle, the General Manager, was demoted and William Chamberlain was 'head-hunted' from Leeds to bring some sort of order to the chaos. An agreement was reached in December at which time the local authority took over most of the vehicles and staff of the bus operators in return for a qualified monopoly of operation within the city and a quarter of a mile beyond.

The 1930s saw the development of trolleybus systems throughout the UK and in 1938 Belfast opened an experimental route on the Falls Road to evaluate this new form of transport. The service was an immediate success and in 1939 the decision was taken gradually to replace all tram routes with trolleybuses.

Although the Second World War significantly slowed down this transition, trolleybuses replaced trams on the Cregagh, Castlereagh, Stormont and Dundonald routes during the War, Belfast having been given government permission to do so. This was almost unique in the UK and was in recognition of Belfast's contribution to the war effort. Following the cessation of hostilities, the Bloomfield route was converted in 1946, Ormeau in 1949 and Greencastle in 1950. By this time economics dictated that diesel buses were cheaper to operate than trolleybuses and all remaining tram routes were converted to bus operation in the early 1950s. The last tram ran from Queen's Road to Ardoyne via High Street and Shankill Road on 28 February 1954.

A couple of interesting sidelines to the story concern the Glengormley and Queen's Road routes. When the Belfast Corporation purchased the C&W, the package included the land at Bellevue which had been developed as pleasure gardens and which was a popular location for evening strolls. There was a proposal, unfortunately not carried out, to build a tramway from the existing Antrim Road line to McArt's Fort at Cavehill. The inherited land at Bellevue was later developed by the BCT as a zoo and became a venue for family outings.

The Queen's Road route was built and owned by the Belfast Harbour Commissioners (BHC) and the traction poles were adorned with the BHC coat of arms, rather than those of the Belfast Corporation which appeared throughout the rest of the system. When shipbuilding was at its height the Queen's Road enjoyed the highest peak period tram service of anywhere in the UK.

The Vehicles

The initial batch of electric trams consisted of 170 identical four-wheel open-toppers from Brush, quickly supplemented by fifty horse cars converted to electric traction. As the routes increased before the First World War, further batches of cars were built by the Tramways Department in Sandy Row Depot. Collectively, these all became known as 'Standard Reds'. Following experiments with top covers, new cars were fitted with them as built and the existing fleet was almost entirely refitted too. Only Nos. 244 to 250 missed being covered and remained open topped until the end of their days. One ex-horse car, No. 249, is preserved in the Ulster Folk and Transport Museum at Cultra, together with horse tram No. 118 and Chamberlain No. 357.

As patronage of the trams increased dramatically – from thirty million per year in 1906 to seventy-four million in 1919 – it was obviously necessary to increase the size of the fleet and in 1920 fifty new cars were supplied by Brush. These new trams became known as 'Moffetts' after the General Manager of the time.

The number of people using the trams increased to 102 million in 1927 and a further fifty cars were ordered from Brush who, in the end, supplied forty while the Belfast-based Service Motor Works built ten. These were the 'Chamberlains', also named after the then General Manager.

The final expansion to the fleet took place in 1935 when a further fifty cars were ordered from English Electric. Designed as 'streamliners' (the generic name given to 'modern' trams of the 1930s which had less angular bodies, with curves to the front and rooflines), they followed tradition and acquired the name 'McCrearys' after the General Manager, Major (later Colonel) McCreary. Although about five years younger, they were outlived by the Chamberlains.

The Photographs

The first two photographs in the book (inside front cover and page one) show examples of the old horse cars and the following five were taken to illustrate the inauguration of the new electric system. The remainder of the photographs are generally laid out in geographical order, showing city centre views first, followed by East Belfast, South Belfast, West Belfast and North Belfast. After that the next pictures show Shore Road and Antrim Road depots, as well as a tram caught in a political demonstration. Finally, there is a small selection of trams posed outside the main works at Sandy Row.

To all of the photographers whose work is represented, I offer my thanks. They were men whose foresight and vision have preserved precious memories for us all to enjoy today.

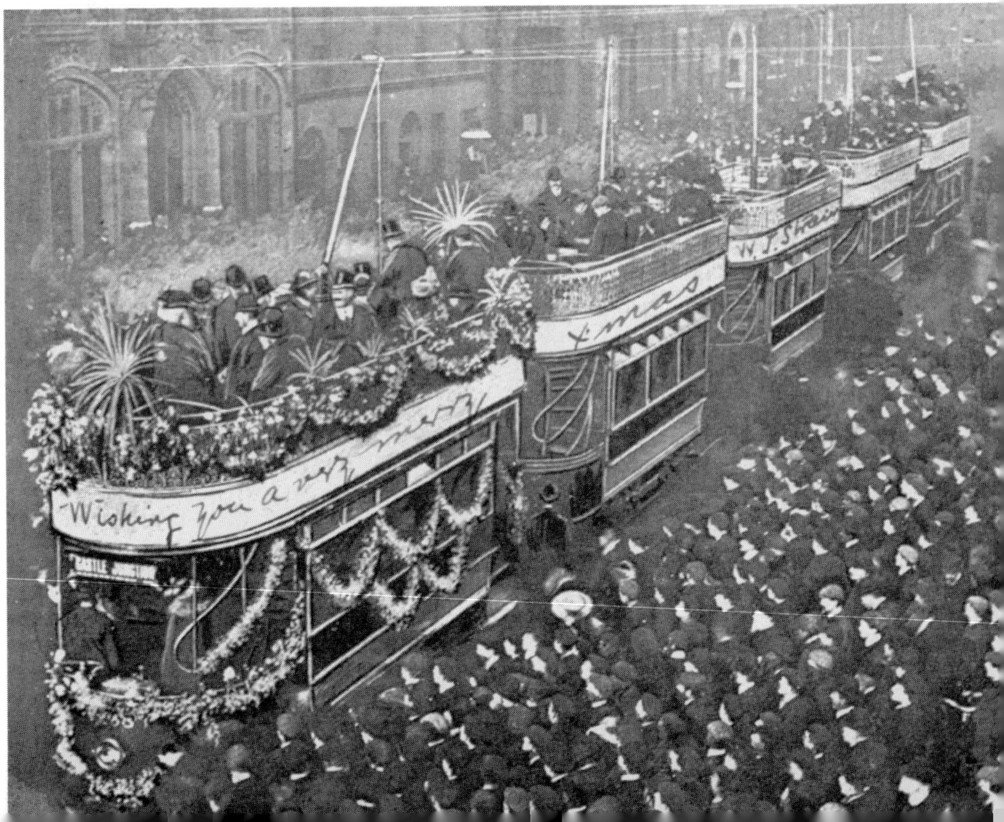

Right: The Southern Routes were opened for electric traction on 29 November 1905. This photograph shows a procession of six cars, led by No. 108, in the city centre on that date. The Lord Mayor, Sir Daniel Dixon, drove the inaugural car from the City Hall to Malone Road, as far as Cranmore Park. Sir Daniel was overheard to remark, 'this is as good as hunting!' The leading car was also filled with local dignitaries. Initially, the overhead traction wires were supported by standards located between the tracks in the centre of the streets (as in this picture), but by 1910 the amount of traffic in the city centre had grown considerably and the decision was taken to locate the poles on the pavement and support the wire carrying the current by span wires. The new cars were 28 feet (8.6 metres) long and 6 feet 10 inches (2.1 metres) wide. The bodies were oak-framed with steel corner plates. The three large windows were glazed with ¼ inch (6 millimetre) plate glass. Downstairs seating was longitudinal, while the upstairs seats were of the 'garden-seat' type. The trucks were Brill 21E types fitted with two 35 horsepower motors. One of these standard cars was displayed at the Brush Company's stand at the 1905 Tramways Exhibition in London. This photograph is heavily retouched, the upper panels being inscribed, 'Wishing You A Merry Xmas W.J. Strain.' (Strain was probably a producer of such postcards at the time).

As part of the opening celebrations No. 66 was decorated with over 1,650 electric lights and travelled around that part of the system which was then open. Passengers were carried at a fare of 6*d*. Remembering that many working people were paid around 3*d* per hour, a trip on the illuminated tram must have seemed rather a luxury! No. 66 was decorated with the city motto on the decency panels, with shamrocks at the corners and the undertaking's monogram at each top deck end. The top deck itself carried lots of assorted greenery and the trolley standard had light bulbs along its entire length. The term 'decency board' referred to the panels which ran the length of the upper deck and were there to protect the decency of female passengers. It was not considered fitting for female ankles to be visible to 'the man in the street' below.

No. 108 was decorated for the occasion of the opening of the electric service on the Southern Routes in November 1905 and is seen here leading a small procession of trams on the Malone Road. Note the advertisements for Van Houten's Cocoa along the side of the top deck and Eoline Calf Meal above the driver; the question of whether or not to allow advertising on trams exercised the Tramways Committee for many years. Eventually commercial considerations won over aesthetic ones and limited advertising was permitted on the side and end panels, on the stair risers, and on the inside windows. However, advertisements for strong drink, though common when the Belfast Street Tramways owned the trams, were banned for many years by the Belfast Corporation.

The first electric cars went into service without top covers, but passengers much preferred to cram into the lower saloon rather than face the driving rain and sleet which often occurred during the winter months. In bad weather some passengers chose to wait for another car rather than face the ordeal, with understandable consequences on the running schedules! In 1907 the Corporation took the decision experimentally to fit several cars with different designs of top covers and No. 257 was one of these. The final design chosen was similar to the one given to this tram (unfortunately, just out of shot), but had a different arrangement of horizontal window bars in the top saloon. Eventually, the entire fleet was fitted with top covers with the exception of ex-horse cars (Nos. 244 to 250) which remained open-topped until the end of their days. By the time this photograph was taken, cars had been fitted with additional destination boxes over the entrances, here clearly showing the cross-town link 'Antrim Road – Ormeau Road via Duncairn Gdns, Bridge Street and Bedford Street'. On the middle side window a route board confirms this and inside the list of penny and twopenny fare stages is displayed.

This and the following two photographs show trams in Donegall Place in the city centre at various times. This view, taken from what is now known as Castle Junction (which was only ever a tramway term, never an address), shows the Hibernia horse bus awaiting passengers for Chichester Park on the Antrim Road. Both it and the double-deck horse tram heading down Donegall Place, towards the White Linen Hall (where the City Hall now stands), were known as 'knifeboards' because of the top deck longitudinal seat which resembled the household implement of the same name. The route details painted on the board above the windows reads 'ANTRIM ROAD CARLISLE CIRCUS HIGH STREET' and the sticker in the middle window also reads 'ANTRIM ROAD'. In 1884 Royal Avenue was opened as a unified development (i.e. the buildings all conformed to regulations on their height to give a unified appearance), replacing the old Hercules and John streets, and by April 1885 tram track had been laid along it, forming a double junction with the existing Castle Place – Donegall Place line. The single gas light in the middle of the road had also been replaced by the much more ornate fitting seen here. The two-storey building on the right was Anderson & McAuley's department store. It was later rebuilt to become the five-storey building illustrated in the next photograph. Lindsay Brothers' warehouse is next door towards the Linen Hall and this was later absorbed into Anderson & McAuley's.

This photograph is rather difficult to date accurately, but was probably taken shortly after the First World War judging by the absence of enclosed trams, the early taxicab and the dress of the pedestrians. Unfortunately, the woman striding purposefully across the street obscures the fleet number of the tram, but it is clearly one of the early standard cars which was top covered in the early 1900s. It is en route to Ligoniel. Anderson & McAuley's building, just behind the tram, acquired three more storeys under the supervision of Young & McKenzie just before the end of the nineteenth century. Both this building and the Bank Buildings store next door, at the right edge of the picture, still stand, albeit no longer operated by their original owners. Further down Donegall Place, Belfast's City Hall can be seen. Sir Alfred Brunwell Thomas built this between 1896 and 1906. Described by Marcus Patton in *Central Belfast* as 'an exuberant wedding cake of a building', it is laid out around a courtyard. The cost of £360,000 was largely funded from the profits of the city's gas department.

Another view down Donegall Place, giving a clearer view of the City Hall and showing a Chamberlain car on the left, Moffett No. 304 and a double-decker bus on the Balmoral to Strandtown service which operated via Donegall Place and High Street. The majority of the buildings on the left-hand side of Donegall Place are still there, and in the left background the photograph shows the towering block of Robinson & Cleaver's store at the corner of Donegall Place and Donegall Square North. Lilliput, advertised on the side of the Chamberlain, was among almost twenty commercial laundries in Belfast (which also included Monarch, Castlereagh, Glen and Globe) which operated fleets of delivery vans.

This view of High Street dates from between 1905 and 1911. The range of buildings on the left-hand side has changed greatly. The Luftwaffe demolished all the buildings between Pollands the Jewellers at No. 18 (the small three-storey building with the second-storey triangular window pediments) and the National Bank at No. 68. In its day the National was by far the tallest building in High Street; today the fifteen-storey River House dwarfs it. Although before the War Bridge Street, running off High Street, was extremely narrow, a double track junction turned into it and led to Donegall Street. Today, Bridge Street is dual carriageway. A modern redbrick building, designed by Young & McKenzie and formerly owned by the Electricity Board for Northern Ireland, replaced the elegant 1860s Arnotts department store (the building on the left-hand side with the cupola).

This photograph was probably taken in the early 1930s, judging by the single Moffett tram among at least six Standard Reds. The buildings on the left-hand side are virtually unaltered from the earlier picture, but on the right edge of the picture, Foster Green's tea and coffee warehouse has been replaced by the Woolworth's/Burton's building, completed in 1930 by Woolworth's in-house construction department. This building is still extant, although occupied by the Internacionale store. Even in the relatively short period separating these pictures, a significant increase in motor vehicles is obvious. From before the First World War, the original Standard Reds had begun to be fitted with top covers. However, the design adopted by Belfast was a saloon-style which enclosed only about one third of the top deck, leaving large open areas at either end. Thus, while a roof ran the length of the tramcar, only very limited protection was available. By the 1920s a number of the Standard Reds had been fitted with route number blinds at upper saloon roof level. All the Moffetts had been fitted with these since their introduction.

Chamberlain No. 376 is heading out of town on High Street, while unidentified Moffett and McCreary cars are going towards Castle Junction in this late 1930s shot. Although I have been unable to identify the date precisely, the presence of the streamlined McCreary car puts it at 1935 or later, while the absence of trolleybus wires means it cannot have been taken later than February 1941. The presence of the shops between Francis Curley's and the National Bank further down High Street also confirms it as pre-Blitz (1941). The Albert Clock can be seen to be leaning a little to the right! This is widely thought to be the result of it being built on reclaimed land. The design was the result of a competition which was won by W.J. Barré, with the well-known local firm of Lanyon, Lynn & Lanyon coming second. The General Purposes Committee in charge of the project reversed this decision, but it subsequently emerged that Lanyon, a Belfast MP, was present when this decision was made. Public outrage forced another U-turn and Barré was given the commission.

Standard Reds Nos. 34 and 116 are seen here in Royal Avenue, beside the Provincial Bank on the left, sometime between 1905 and 1910. Both cars are still open topped and No. 34 is on its way to Clintonville, while No. 116 is en route to Malone Road. At junctions on the system, such as here at Castle Junction, there was a clear order of precedence for trams, with inbound cars taking priority over outbound ones; where two inbound cars from different routes met, there was a table of precedence. For example, at Royal Avenue/North Street, visible in the distance, cars going towards Castle Junction via Royal Avenue had right of way over those coming from North Street. The Royal Avenue Hotel on the right was demolished in 1984 to be replaced by the four-storey red brick building, Avenue House. The canopy outside the hotel was removed some time before that. Among its famous guests were Louis Armstrong and Ella Fitzgerald. The Grand Central Hotel, once Belfast's premier hotel and which can be identified three blocks down on the left by its rounded corner, was closed in the 1960s (it was later an army base for a time before becoming part of the Castle Court shopping complex). Included among its guests were Sir Winston Churchill and Al Jolson. Next door, the Workshops for the Industrious Blind and the General Post Office were also both demolished in 1985 to make way for the glass and concrete Castle Court.

This view of No. 15 on its way to Balmoral was taken in Castle Place in the early twentieth century and shows three other top covered cars in Castle Junction. The large building to the left, 2.4.6 The Castle, was Leahy, Kelly & Leahy's tobacco warehouse and was replaced in 1970 by the present four-storey Dolcis building. The Bank Buildings block facing the camera is still standing, although currently owned by Primark, while Robb's grand five-storey department store on the right was demolished to make way for Donegall Arcade in 1989/90. Robb's had been on this site since 1861, gradually expanding until by 1920 it occupied the entire block. Regrettably, it ceased trading in 1973. The stop sign on the traction pole nearest the camera on the left read 'Cars Stop By Request'; the words 'Cars' and 'By Request' were in white lettering on a blue background, while 'Stop' (in much larger lettering) was black on white. The three horizontal bands on the traction pole behind denoted an overhead insulator, which separated one electrical section from another. If the motorman failed to knock off the power when passing an insulator, he would risk damaging the equipment.

Queen's Road, Belfast, was essentially an industrial tram route, provided mainly for the workers of Harland & Wolff, which at its peak employed nearly 30,000 men and was the largest shipyard in the world. In 1908 the Belfast Harbour Commissioners laid a tram route from Station Street, beside the terminus of the Belfast & County Down Railway, to the junction of Queen's Road and Thompson Wharf Road, and it was their coat of arms which was carried on the traction poles. The line, though owned by the BHC, was always worked by the Belfast City Tramways. Centre poles supported the overhead until the route was abandoned to buses in 1954. One unusual feature was that a short section of tramway overhead was easily detachable to allow the transfer of large loads (e.g. ships' boilers and propellers) from one side of the shipyard to the other.

This picture is reproduced from a postcard dated 1923, though judging from the people's dress and the total absence of motor traffic it was probably taken some time before then. The large church to the right is Saint Patrick's Church of Ireland and the tram is just about to pass St Leonard's Street on its left on its way to Belmont. Redevelopment has changed much of this scene. The horse-drawn delivery cart was owned by Wilson & Montgomery who had premises not only on the Newtownards Road but also on the Castlereagh Road. The advertisement for Kelly's Stout on the gable wall just behind the tram to the right was typical of the enthusiasm with which brewers advertised their products in those days!

This picture was taken some time after trams had given way to trolleybuses in East Belfast in the 1940s. The wires going to the left are for trolleybuses heading to Holywood Road, Belmont and Stormont, while those leading (more or less) straight on are for Knock and Dundonald. The Holywood Arches, as this area is known, took its name from the railway bridges that spanned both the Holywood and Newtownards Roads and carried the Belfast & County Down Railway to Newtownards, Comber, Newcastle and Downpatrick. Shortly after this line was abandoned in 1950, the bridges were partly demolished, leaving the remains seen in the picture. One part of the bridge support protruded quite a way into the Newtownards Road, causing a significant bottleneck to traffic for many years. All traces of the bridges have now been removed. The shops nearest the camera have been rebuilt in a similar style to that shown and the large suburban terraced housing on the Newtownards Road is largely unchanged today. The bus near the middle of the picture, probably No. 535 (registration number HGC261), was one of 100 wartime Daimlers purchased from London Transport in 1953/54 to speed up the tram replacement project. They were initially pressed into service in their original London bodywork (slightly modified), but all were later re-bodied by Harkness Coachworks. Although apparently very similar to the 'standard' Belfast body, the ex-London vehicles could be distinguished by the single top deck rear window and top deck front windows with inward opening ventilation panes.

Moffett No. 332, photographed on the Newtownards Road on the Dundonald – Antrim Road service. While it is not possible to date the photograph accurately, judging by the ladies' clothing, motor vehicles, and the style of the fleet number numerals on the tram, it was possibly taken in the early 1930s. In the centre of the picture the rear of a single-deck bus can just be seen. The street to the left beside the tram is Bloomfield Avenue. The bus is close to the Albertbridge Road junction, which provided an alternative route into the city centre for trams, later trolleybuses, and still does for motorbuses. Stormont and Dundonald services operate on both legs of the route. The buildings beside the 'STOP' sign remain in modernised form, with shop fronts, while the tea and coffee shop on the far corner of Bloomfield Avenue has been replaced by Wise Buys. The remainder of the buildings on the left as far as Albertbridge Road have all been demolished, and the shops on the right, including, regrettably, the barrel clock, have also been replaced by modern shops. The gaslights here are a rather elegant hexagonal shape, though unusually without the short horizontal ladder support. By this time most of the lights worked automatically with pilot jets and clockwork mechanisms, which required periodic winding.

Standard Red No. 42 begins the climb from Holywood Arches to Gelston's Corner (the junction of the Holywood and Belmont roads) early last century. The buildings containing Gilbey's Wine Lodge and William Fisher's furniture shop are still present, albeit under different ownership. The small railway-like houses next to Fisher's have been replaced by a doctors' surgery and an electrical shop. The three-storey houses just behind the tram are still in place today. The hoarding to the right has long since been removed and the space is currently occupied by the single-storey Park Vale Discount Stores and another two-storey shop. The advertisement on the front of the tram for Inglis' Bread referred to a famous (and not very long extinct) local bakery whose main building was on the Newtownards Road, only a short distance from the site of the photograph. The street to the left is Madison Avenue East, while on the right is Grampian Street.

No. 223 was on the Holywood Road, at the corner of Connsbrook Avenue heading towards Belmont, when this photograph was taken early last century. The large terraced houses on the left, while modernised and changed to some degree, are entirely recognisable today, while the vacant ground to the right is currently occupied by relatively new developments, including a new police station. In the distance is the hall formerly used by the Ulster Unionist Association (it appears in close-up in the next picture). The photograph also shows the elegant traction poles adopted in the early days of electric trams. The span wire was attached to ornamental scrollwork on the traction poles, which were fitted with collars at two places. They also had ornamental cast iron bases embellished with the city's coat of arms. Regrettably, much of this ornamentation disappeared over the years.

Still in East Belfast, Standard Red No. 112 makes its way up Belmont Road. It is not possible to be precise about the date of the photograph, but the road is considerably narrower than at present, while the large building with the curved front is still there, minus its cupola. For many years it housed Strandtown and District Unionist Club and Victoria Unionist Association. The Stormont Inn has replaced Tedford's Posting Establishment. The terraces of houses on the right of the picture remain today, though without their entrance porches. The small street to the right is Dundela Crescent, while the road to the left is the continuation of Holywood Road, which never had a tram service. After the Second World War, a motorbus service operated along Holywood Road as far as Garnerville Road.

Standard Red No. 10, although incorrectly showing 'KNOCK' on its destination blind (probably because the driver and conductor had failed to set it properly!), is actually on the Upper Newtownards Road on its way to Castle Junction. The street to the right is Earlswood Road and the one to the left Hillview Avenue. The corner shop and terrace at Earlswood Road are still present, though were recently re-roofed without their chimneys. Most of the terraced houses fronting the Newtownards Road have had their ground floors converted into shops. The terrace of shops on the left is still there today, albeit with much modernised fronts.

A Moffett tram at the same location as the last picture – Upper Newtownards Road, with the junction for Earlswood Road on the right. There are several early motor cars on the road, and women's fashion has changed quite radically from the full length dress in the earlier picture to the slightly below-the-knee look! The buildings in this picture are little changed from the previous photograph and the traction poles and overhead fittings are also unchanged. The simplified overhead installation came into force during and after the First World War.

For many years Belfast's trams had terminated at the city boundary and displayed 'Knock' on their destination indicators. On 7 July 1924, however, the line was extended to the gates of Dundonald Cemetery, where this unidentified Moffett was photographed 'at the end of the lines'. The scene is still very much recognisable today, although there have been changes. The current Maxol filling station is where the shop used to be and Robb's garage has been replaced by a car salesroom. The telephone box has gone, but the trees on the right have survived.

An unidentified top covered Standard Red heads into town along the Ravenhill Road, probably before the First World War. The street nearest to the camera is Florida Street and the two terraces of houses to the right of the picture are very little changed today, apart from several trees growing in the front gardens. The wall and railings to the extreme right belong to Ravenhill Presbyterian Church.

Standard Red No. 139, right, en route to Donegall Road. The photograph was taken after 1913, when Shaftesbury Square became a very complicated tramway junction with two lines entering from the north and three leaving from the south. The track was laid so that cars could work from either Great Victoria Street or Dublin Road to Botanic Avenue, Bradbury Place or Donegall Road. The sweep of McCusker's Family Grocer shop on the left has been replaced several times and is currently a building site, but the vista up Botanic Avenue is still recognisable, albeit with ground floor shops. However, some of the terrace nearest the camera has been demolished to make room for Save the Children Fund offices and a Chinese carry-out. The main curved building in the centre of the picture, Ferris Brothers', has been replaced by the Northern Bank, although without the circular fourth-floor windows and chimneys. The white painted standards in the middle and extreme right of the photograph denote the position of insulators in the overhead wiring. By law all tramways were required to have their overhead traction wires split into half-mile sections for safety reasons.

This photograph looks north, towards the city centre. Standard Red No. 1 is on the Stranmillis Road to Northern Counties Railway via Great Victoria Street route, and it is clear from the picture that tracks have not yet been laid in Botanic Avenue, putting the picture before January 1913. When the tramways were electrified in 1905, the only routes south of Shaftesbury Square were along Bradbury Place and University Road, or branching right to the Lisburn Road and Sandy Row Depot. North of the Square, trams could reach the city centre either by the original route along Great Victoria Street and Wellington Place or via Dublin Road and Bedford Street. In the early 1930s Shaftesbury Square was made into a 'gyratory' system of traffic (except for trams, which went the way they always had – straight across). As motor traffic replaced horse-drawn vehicles this junction became one of the busiest in the city and warranted a permanent police pointsman. For many years in the 1960s Constable Harry White was the regular man, whose sense of humour earned him the nickname 'Smiler'. The three-storey houses and shops on the left of the picture were replaced by Shaftesbury House in 1935. The block on the left further down Great Victoria Street is still there, although there have been changes to the ground floor shops. The little hut and church in the centre of the picture have been swept away to make room for a branch of the Ulster Bank. The block of curved buildings to the right have all been replaced by a rather ugly modern office block.

In this photograph Standard Red No. 107 is going in the direction of Stranmillis Terminus, in spite of the destination indicator reading 'N.C.R.Y.' (Northern Counties Railway). It is possible that the crew had not set the correct display at the previous terminus or that they had set it for the return journey too soon. The scene at Stranmillis Road has not changed a great deal today, all the buildings visible in the photograph still being present. The trees on the left-hand side of the road have grown in the last seventy or so years, while the railings on the right and at the side were removed during the Second World War and never replaced. The routes to Malone and Stranmillis were built by the Belfast Corporation under their 1899 Act, although they continued to be operated by the Belfast Street Tramways Company until its compulsory purchase by BCT in 1905. In fact, the Stranmillis Route was opened in two stages – in 1899 as far as Ridgeway Street, and in January 1913 to Lockview Road, the terminus being at the first lock.

Standard Red No. 55, photographed making its way up the slight hill near Windsor Avenue on Malone Road. The lack of top cover on the tram strongly suggests a date of before 1912 and the total lack of any traffic, save for a horse-drawn cart, and the design of the street lamps bear this out. The spire on the right belongs to Fisherwick Presbyterian Church, which was built to replace the original Presbyterian church in Fisherwick Place (the original church was demolished to make way for the Presbyterian Assembly Buildings around 1905). The stone wall to the left now has a footpath alongside and the trees on the right have grown quite a lot; otherwise the scene has not radically changed.

This photograph shows the Donegall Road Terminus, at its junction with the Falls Road, where McCreary No. 406 is awaiting departure for Antrim Road via Great Victoria Street. In the background No. 416 is about to reverse over the crossover, bound for Ligoniel. The McCreary cars were introduced from 1935 and were named after the General Manager of the time, Major Robert McCreary. A minority of the cars (fleet Nos. 392 and 423–441) were built by English Electric, but the rest (Nos. 393–422) were constructed to an almost identical design by Service Motor Works in Belfast. The two batches can be distinguished by the position of the headlights. The Service cars' headlights were in the 'low' position (i.e. about midway up the dash), while the English Electric cars had theirs mounted at the top of the dash, just below the fleet number. Fleet Nos. 392 and 393 were fitted with separate drivers' cabs (i.e. they had a door between the driver's compartment and the passengers' area), but this feature wasn't continued in either production batch. Other features of the new cars were of course the streamlining (McCreary trams were often known as 'streamliners'), an all-metal body, and entrance doors. Over the doors a comprehensive destination display was provided, comprising destination, route and route number information, in addition to the destination and route number displays at either end. The press handout at the time proudly boasted that the display on these cars exceeded that of London! This photograph was taken over sixty years ago, but the scene has changed little. A number of the trees were cut down for use as barricades during the riots of 1969, but they have largely grown back since then.

In 1928 a 'war' broke out between private bus owners and the Corporation trams and this lasted from June to December. The General Manager, Samuel Carlisle, was forced to step down and was replaced by William Chamberlain from Leeds. Although he stayed only two years, Chamberlain made sweeping changes, including the ordering of new cars and the rebuilding of fifty Standard Reds. No. 263 was one of this class of rebuilt cars, which had improved motors, enclosed top decks, upholstered seating and were painted in the new Princess blue and white livery. For some reason most of the fifty cars, including this one, had 'uneven' window heights, with deeper windows in the centre of the upper saloon. A small number, however, had the much more elegant 'same height' windows all round. Essentially, the rebuilt cars looked like shortened Chamberlains. The basic road layout at the Springfield Road Terminus has barely changed, though the open ground behind the fence in the middle picture is now occupied by modern housing, which also replaces the terrace of three-storey houses to the right of the tram. The little iron construction to the right of the tram is a gents' toilet, built at many tram termini. Basic in the extreme, it nevertheless provided a very necessary function in the days when twelve-hour days without relief were common.

McCreary No. 397 at Ballygomartin Terminus in July 1939, with Moffett No. 325 waiting its turn to use the crossover. The cottage to the left of the McCreary has been demolished, but the housing just behind the Moffett is still present today. The wall to the extreme right of the picture encloses Forth River Primary School.

In this July 1939 photograph, Standard Red No. 2 has just arrived from the city centre and is about to reverse over the crossover at Ardoyne, preparatory to operating a shipyard special to Queen's Road. The view of the hills in the centre background is largely unchanged today, but a large housing estate was constructed in the middle distance in the 1950s. Ardoyne Depot, which was opened in 1913 at the same time as the extensions to Stranmillis, Ligoniel, Donegall Road, Bloomfield, Castlereagh and Botanic Avenue were constructed, lay just out of sight to the right. It was approached by a very steep curve and was entered via a red brick arch originally incorporating an elegant clock. After the trams were abandoned in 1954 it became a bus depot and a large parking yard was built beside it. That too has been demolished and replaced by modern housing. The only former tram depot currently operational (as a municipal transport depot) is Falls Park, which was one of the original horse-car depots.

The next two photographs were taken very close together at the Ligoniel Terminus. This photograph of open topper No. 246 appeared on a postcard dated 2 September 1939, and judging from the contemporary dress I would say that the date is probably accurate. No. 246 was one of the fifty original horse cars converted to electric traction after 1905 and one of seven never to receive a top cover. Rebuilt in the period before the First World War to look like the original 170 Brush cars, the ex-horse cars could be distinguished by the deeper waist panel and shallower rocker panel (the side panel immediately above the wheels), as well as being significantly shorter. The houses and shop to the left of the tram have been demolished to make way for modern housing, the stone toilet for the convenience of the tram crews has been dismantled and Mill Avenue, into which the track went, has been realigned. When the Ligoniel extension from St Mark's Church was opened in 1913, after a lot of public pressure, it was felt that the handbrake might be insufficient to hold the cars safely on the steep Ligoniel Road and the track was laid into the relatively flat Mill Avenue. Initially, two crossovers were laid in, perhaps with the intention of shunting cars easily, but they eventually fell into disuse. After the introduction of air braked cars, trams waited on the Ligoniel Road itself.

McCreary No. 432 in July 1939. The village of Ligoniel once boasted its own tramway, linking St Mark's Church to the then terminus of the Belfast Street Tramways at Flax Street on the Crumlin Road. The Ligoniel Company, although separately owned and financed, was worked by the BST which used its own staff and rolling stock; the BST retained the fares and paid an annual rental. The mill village of Ligoniel always considered itself as being independent from Belfast and for many years 'kept itself to itself'. The terminal layout is interesting in that after the two tracks merged, they diverged again and a further crossover was provided, the route ending in a double stub. The layout is visible in the picture. It is not clear what the purpose for this rather elaborate – and for Belfast unique – terminal arrangement was, but I presume that there was the expectation (or at least hope) of very heavy traffic from the mills. So far as I am aware the additional crossovers were not used; they were later removed.

Ex-horse car No. 232 photographed at the Cliftonville Road Terminus in the early part of last century. The scene today has not radically changed, although the two gaps to the left and right have since been filled in. Almost all the houses in the picture are still standing, though a number have had ground floor shop fronts fitted. The street to the left is Ashgrove Park. The spire in the centre of the picture belongs to Oldpark Presbyterian Church, while the gap on the right-hand side of Cliftonville Road is filled with two-storey shops and semi-detached houses. Although not visible in this picture, there was a route down the Oldpark Road with which the Cliftonville trams shared a common terminus. At that time Cliftonville cars worked across the city to Ormeau Road.

Chamberlain No. 344, Moffett No. 295 and an unidentified tram at Cliftonville Terminus in July 1939. The Chamberlain had just had its trolley turned before heading across town to Castlereagh Road. The Moffett had arrived via Oldpark Road and would return to Bloomfield. By the early 1930s a great deal of new housing had been built beyond the tram terminus. The street to the left is Westland Road and that to the right, Alliance Avenue. It was never served by trams or trolleybuses, but the bus service which began in the 1960s was often suspended by civil disturbances. On 12 February 1934, a new bus service was opened to the Ballysillan Road and the bus stop sign can be seen to the right of the picture.

Although this photograph, taken on Antrim Road beside the waterworks, cannot be dated precisely, judging from the state of dress, and the tram not yet being top covered, it was probably taken before the First World War. The little gate lodge to the left of the picture is still there today, as are the (now extensively refurbished) houses to the right. Most of them have been converted into ground floor shops, of the fast food and off-licence variety. The policeman on the right-hand pavement is in the uniform of the Royal Irish Constabulary. This was replaced in 1922 by the Royal Ulster Constabulary and a similar force in the then Free State. Perhaps it is a sign of more peaceful times in Northern Ireland when one policeman was able to patrol alone.

This photograph was taken at Glengormley Terminus early last century. The camera was facing the city centre. In horse car days, Belfast Street Tramways never got beyond Chichester Park on the Antrim Road and to supplement the Belfast cars, an independent operator known as the Cavehill & Whitewell Tramway Company opened a line from Chichester Park to Glengormley, variously using steam, horse and latterly electric traction. In 1911 the Belfast Corporation purchased the C&W undertaking and, in addition to the cars, depot and other plant, acquired lands at Glengormley and Bellevue on which was eventually built the city's zoo. A recruitment office and a building society have replaced the Glengormley Arms and next-door café. A major suburban junction, complete with traffic lights and pedestrian barriers, has replaced the general air of a quiet country village that existed eighty years ago.

This photograph was taken further up the Antrim Road in the direction of the city centre some years after the previous one and shows an enclosed car, which dates it to after 1928. The garage to the left has been moved to make way for a modern garage, itself currently derelict and fenced off. On the right-hand side the trees are no longer there, having been cut down to make way for a furniture shop and warehouse.

This shot was taken in Duncairn Gardens in July 1939. Traditionally, the Antrim Road routes were served by both Carlisle Circus and Duncairn Gardens and this was maintained right through trolleybus days and, to a more limited degree, this is still the situation. This area is totally changed, with none of the buildings shown still standing. Chamberlain No. 366 has just crossed North Queen Street from Brougham Street and is about to climb Duncairn Gardens. The 'ALL CARS STOP HERE' sign can be seen at the junction, as can the old-style crossing.

Standard Red No. 144 and another in York Street feature in this photograph which was probably taken before the First World War, judging from the clothing and lack of motor vehicles. No. 144 is bound for Antrim Road (via Duncairn Gardens) while the tram in the other direction is headed for the Falls Road. At this time (and for very many years afterwards) the Greencastle tram route was linked with the Falls Road. The link was suspended from 1938 (when the Falls trolleybuses started), but restored in 1950 when Whitehouse trolleybuses took over from the trams. None of the buildings on either side of the street survive today. The street between the *Sunday Chronicle* advertisement and the Co-op building was York Lane. The narrow street to the right is Curtis Street. The Luftwaffe demolished almost all the buildings on the right-hand side of York Street in 1941; the government later demolished the few that survived. The Co-op building on the left was replaced by the present structure in 1936, and this was sold to the University of Ulster as residential accommodation. The same university occupies most of the right-hand side of this part of York Street, in a building formerly known as the College of Art and Design.

The next two photographs show the Northern Counties Railway Station in the first decade of the last century and here open topper No. 52 was photographed on its way to Greencastle. The destination indicator shows 'GREENCASTLE (SHORE RD)' and the photograph, though undated is pre-First World War by which time No. 52 had been top covered and the central traction poles replaced by side poles and span wires. Like the previous photograph, very little of this scene remains today. The railway station and all the surrounding houses were redeveloped at various times, but the major factor in the changes was the construction of the foreshore M2 Motorway.

If the station clock is accurate, Standard Red No. 2 was about to return to Castle Junction at 4.30 p.m. This photograph from July 1939 shows the elegant Northern Counties Railway Station, before it was severely damaged in the Blitz of 1941. Although not unique, Belfast was unusual in having tram bays into two of its main line railway stations. There was a ten-minute service from Castle Junction to the LMS railway station via Corporation Street linked with the Stranmillis service. This was in addition to the regular service to Greencastle, which passed the station, and the Antrim Road via Duncairn Gardens service, which passed close by. However, the track layout was such that trams scheduled to enter the bay had to approach via York Street. Before the days of trams, the line was called the Belfast & Ballymena Railway, later becoming the Belfast & Northern Counties Railway to reflect its geographical expansion. On 1 July 1903 it became part of the Midland Railway. In 1923, as a result of the mainland amalgamations, it became the London, Midland & Scottish Railway (Northern Counties Committee) as shown by the sign. Trams and buses showed destinations variously as 'Northern Counties Railway', 'LM&S Railway, 'LMS Rly NCC' and 'N.C. Railway', and not always appropriate to what was the actual name at any given time!

Although this picture cannot accurately be dated, it was probably taken before the First World War. The view is of Greencastle village, a place not reached by the trams until 1905. The houses and shop premises on the left-hand side of the picture still stand although all the dwellings beyond the traction pole have been demolished, as have all the whitewashed cottages on the right. Two major flyovers of the M2 motorway dominate this area.

An unusual view, taken inside Antrim Road Depot, of Standard Red top-covered No. 64, rebuild No. 252 and ex-horse car No. 244. No. 64 wears a plate saying 'NOT TO GO OUT', while No. 252 carries an advertisement for the local bakery firm of Inglis. No. 244 was one of the seven ex-horse cars never to receive a top cover and as such was used mainly on Bellevue specials in the summer. The Bellevue land was acquired by the Belfast Corporation as part of the purchase agreement of the Cavehill & Whitewell Tramway in 1911 and was later developed into the zoo. However, for many years it was administered by the Tramways (later Transport) Department and became a favourite destination for a family day out right into the 1960s. On bank holidays and weekends as many trams as could be made available were pressed into service.

Only recently demolished, Shore Road Depot was opened in 1905 to serve the electrified system and the new extensions (e.g. Greencastle and Duncairn Gardens). The partly obscured tram to the left is No. 89, which was unique in the fleet. In the early 1920s various experiments were carried out to cover in the old partially top covered trams (like No. 121). No. 89 was one attempt and not repeated. However, she retained this one-off top cover for the rest of her days. The finished look was rather top-heavy and she acquired the nickname 'Queen Mary' as a result. One of the main grumbles of the motormen were that the design of the top deck made the rain pour into their (unprotected) driving position!

From the late nineteenth century a movement took root in Ireland for independence from the rest of Britain. However, the majority of people in the north-east part of Ireland strongly objected to the idea, believing they would be much better off remaining part of the UK. During the 'debates', the discussion got very heated and passionate and lots of speakers came to address meetings who were both 'pro' and 'anti' Home Rule. On one occasion, in 1912, Mr (later Sir) Winston Churchill came to address a 'pro' Home Rule meeting, but was angrily booed and jeered and forced to move the venue of his meeting from the Ulster Hall (a Unionist venue) to Celtic Park (where nationalist support could be counted on). This photograph, taken in the city centre, shows the crowd, complete with placards opposed to Home Rule and a Union flag. The tram, which is unidentified, was intending to go to Queen's Road.

This photograph was taken in Gaffikin Street, one of the entrances to Sandy Row Depot. The entire area has been demolished and replaced by modern housing and a factory. The footpath between the tram and the houses was little more than 2 feet wide (approximately 60 centimetres). No. 78 was one of fifty cars rebuilt by William Chamberlain in 1928–30 and to all intents and purposes it was a cut-down edition of the Chamberlain cars. The obvious distinguishing feature was that the 'proper' Chamberlain cars had four windows in the lower saloon, as opposed to the 'Rebuilds' which had three. The 'Rebuild' class had their wheelbases extended from 6 feet 6 inches to 7 feet 6 inches. The handrails were covered in vulcanite and the motors up rated from 2 x 30 to 2 x 50 horsepower. The fleet livery was changed from red and white to Princess blue and white and the reconditioned cars were delivered in the new colours. This car is unusual in that the upper saloon side windows were the same height all round, while most of the class had deeper windows in the middle with shallower ones to the sides, giving a somewhat eccentric look.

This is ex-horse car No. 211. Initially, it was decided to convert five of the old horse trams to electric traction. However, when the first cars were stripped down they were found to be in such good condition that it was subsequently decided to convert fifty instead. They were numbered 201 to 250. The first 'version' of the converted horse cars was quite distinctive from the Standard Reds. Outside the Standards had decorative scroll work the length of the top deck; the former horse cars did not. The Standards had half-turn staircases; the horse cars had quarter-turn stairs. The Standards had their headlights mounted on the lower dash; the horse cars had theirs mounted on the upper dash panel. The destination boxes on the Standards were mounted below the canopy; those on the horse cars were located near the top of the front upper deck panels. At the time of top-covering most of the fleet, the ex-horse cars were altered to match more closely the Standard Reds and many of the above differences were eliminated. However, the iron grilles at the ends of the dashes were retained. A further distinguishing feature was that the horse cars had shallower rocker panels (the white panels just above the wheels) than the Standards.